Katrin Unterreiner

The Habsburgs

Portrait of a European dynasty

pichler verlag

A FAMILY CONQUERS THE WORLD

The Habsburgs, who reigned for over 640 years as kings and emperors of the Holy Roman Empire and, from 1804, as emperors of Austria until the end of the monarchy in the year 1918, were not only one of the most important dynasties in Europe but also dominated the course of world history for centuries. In keeping with the motto "Tu felix Austria nube!" – "Thou, happy Austria, marry!", mainly due to skilful marriage policies, they created a world empire that spanned the kingdoms of Hungary and Bohemia, through Austria all the way to Spain and across the ocean to the Spanish colonies in South America and "where the sun never set".

In Europe, as well as worldwide, the Habsburgs had politically important roles. From Maria Theresa's daughter Marie Antoinette, who was executed as a French queen, to her sister Maria Carolina of Naples and Sicily, who courageously fought against Napoleon. From Archduchess Marie Louise, who as Napoleon's second wife, gave him heirs, to her sister Maria Leopoldina, who as empress of Brazil is revered as a sovereign even today. The dynasty was at the zenith of its power from the beginning of 16th to the end of the 17th century, when the Habsburgs reigned as Spanish kings and finally, through Charles V, was divided into two lines – the Spanish and Austrian. In addition to the existing colonies in South America, the Spanish Habsburgs not only conquered Peru, Mexico and Florida, but also the Philippines, named after Philip II, and thus built up the worldwide empire of the dynasty.

As well as shaping history, the Habsburgs also shaped European culture. As patrons and avid collectors they promoted arts and science. Their seat of residence Vienna became one of the leading capital cities in Europe. They acted as Catholic emperors during the time of religious wars, and afterwards as the main representatives of the Counter-Reformation, which also found its expression in magnificent buildings. To this day, the Habsburgs are not only omnipresent in the city profile of Vienna – think of the representational buildings that bear their coat of arms and insignias – but also in many institutions that are still known all over the world and which characterise the Austrian tradition. From Maximilian I, going back to the Vienna Boys Choir, to Charles VI, who founded the Spanish Riding School, to Emperor Francis Joseph, who cultivated the culture of the great balls that are immortal even in this day and age. With the end of the monarchy in the year 1918, the rule of the Habsburgs ended, but many of the traditions that date back to them continue to live on today. The "Habsburg myth" is more alive than ever ...

Above: The Habsburg escutcheon from the time of Emperor Charles VI shows the double-headed eagle as a symbol of the Holy Roman Empire, with the coat of arms of the House of Austria as well as Castile, because Spain still then belonged to the world empire of the Habsburgs. The crest of the escutcheon is the crown of the Holy Roman Empire.
Left page: The Hofburg was the main residence of the Habsburgs from the beginning of their reign in Austria in the 13th century up to the end of the monarchy in the year 1918, thus making Vienna the centre of European politics and history for over 640 years.

The coat of arms of the Austro-Hungarian double monarchy.

INSEPARABILITER

H. G. Ströhl

Rudolphus Rom. Rex.

Meinhex Bischoff zu Maintz.

Ludwig Pfaltz graf churfurst.

Seyfrid Bischoff zu Cölln.

Hainrich Bischoff zu Trier.

Albrecht hertzog zu Sachsen Churf.

Herman Marg zu Brand. Churf.

RUDOLF I
THE FOREFATHER

The roots of the Habsburgs lie in today's Switzerland, in the canton Aargau, where the ruins of the Habsburg castle are located. From the beginning, the Habsburgs showed aptitude in increasing their lands and thus their position of power. From a small Aargau estate, the family's domain continually expanded towards South Germany to Alsace. However, what became a deciding factor was Rudolf Habsburg's crowning as King of the Romans in 1273, which would lead to the family's rapid rise as one of Europe's leading dynasties. However, early on, this was far from clear.

In the year 1254, the extinction of the Staufen, who, after the Ottonians and the Salians, had been bestowed with royal and imperial dignity for over a

century, led to decades of disputes over the succession, and kings and rival kings had alternated in short periods. The prince-electors who elected the king had agreed on Rudolf and thus ended the interregnum. But because he came from relatively minor lineage, he had powerful adversaries from the beginning – above all in the form of Ottokar II Przemysl, the powerful king of Bohemia. Following the dying out of the Babenbergs, Ottokar II had appropriated the Austrian countries, which Rudolf did not accept, and thus the decision was taken onto the battle fields.

In 1278, Rudolf conquered Ottokar in the battle on the Marchfeld by Dürnkrut and Jedenspeigen and, with the approval of the electors, enfeoffed his own sons Albrecht and Rudolf with the Austrian hereditary lands. He thus founded the rule of the Habsburgs in Austria, which would last until the end of the monarchy in the year 1918. Vienna became the royal seat, even though Rudolf himself seldom spent time in Vienna. Following Rudolf's death in 1291, his son Albrecht was named his successor, but the election was not unanimous and because at the time still no majority voting system existed, the decision was again taken to battle. Albrecht was able to conquer his rival Adolf of Nassau and rule until he was murdered on 1 May 1308 by his own nephew, Johann "the Parricide". However his son and successor Frederick the Fair had less luck and was outnumbered by his rival, Ludwig of Bavaria, in the new double elections of 1314. This initially signified the loss of the Habsburgs' royal dignity for a long time.

Above: The tomb of King Rudolf I of Habsburg in Speyer Cathedral.
Left page: The coronation of Rudolf I as German king took place on 24 October 1273 in Aachen Cathedral.

In 1282, at the Augsburg Reichstag, King Rudolf I enfeoffed his sons Albrecht and Rudolf with the duchies of Austria, Styria, Carinthia and Carniola and the Windic Mark *(marca Vindica)*.

Above right: The "Habichtsburg", also called "Habspurg", in the canton Aargau in Switzerland. The Habsburgs may have lost their possessions in Switzerland due to the Swiss Confederation founded in 1291 during the 14th century, however they had already moved their centre of rule to the east – to Vienna.

Centre right: The old castle dates back to the Bohemian King Ottokar II Przemysl. The castle, which then had four towers, today comprises the historical core of the Vienna Hofburg, named Schweizertrakt. Following Rudolf I of Habsburg's defeat of Ottokar, the Habsburgs took over his Vienna residence.

Below right: Rudolf of Habsburg conquered King Ottokar of Bohemia in the Battle of Dürnkrut in 1278 and took over the reign of the Austrian territories. Painting by Carl von Blaas, ca. 1868.

RUDOLF IV
FORGER AND FOUNDER

Albrecht's grandson, Duke Rudolf IV (1339–1365), was the first Habsburg duke to be born and grow up in the country – which not only influenced his popularity, but above all decidedly shaped Vienna as his birth town and city of residence. Duke Rudolf IV only reigned for seven years, but these were affected by particularly ambitious intentions. In 1365, he founded the Vienna University, which makes it the oldest university in the German-speaking world; started the construction of the Gothic St. Stephen's cathedral and was able to expand the Austrian territories even more, when, in 1363, due to a contract of inheritance, Tyrol also fell to Austria.

However his most important goal was to increase Austria's eminence and prestige and that of the House of Habsburg. This was done by also using some unorthodox means and, with the *Privilegium Maius*, "forged" one of the most important documents in Austrian history. The reason for this was the slight the Habsburgs received within the empire. They were not included in the Golden Bull of 1356, in which the Bohemian king and Emperor Charles IV had named seven prince-electors who had the right to elect the emperor of the Holy Roman Empire. In order to compensate for this loss of power, in

1358/59 Rudolf had his chancellery forge the so-called *Privilegium Maius*, which was to ensure him with comparable privileges. Included was also the title of archduke, which upgraded the basic duke title of the Habsburgs and would raise him above all other dukes, as well as the right to bear a crown-like insignia – the so-called "archducal hat".

Although the imperial chancellery in Prague immediately recognised the forgery, Charles IV, who was also Rudolf's father-in-law through the Habsburg's marriage to his daughter Katharina, tolerated the carrying of the archduke title, but never endorsed it, which is why it initially remained illegitimate.

However Rudolf not only followed ambitious plans within the empire, but also in the country, and decreed a number of economic and social measures, which he financed with the drinks tax that he had introduced. When Rudolf died childless at the age of 26, his brother Albert III, known as Albert with the Pigtail, inherited the rule. His grandson Albert V even managed to assume royal dignity for a short time (1438–1439). But it wasn't until two generations later that the Habsburgs were able to rise to a dynasty, whose power extended beyond Europe to the New World.

Above: Under Rudolf IV, the new gothic building of the landmark of the city of Vienna, St. Stephen's Cathedral, was begun. Rudolf's sobriquet "the Founder" comes from Rudolf's own secret code engraved on the building, which identifies him as a church founder.
Left page: The portrait of Rudolf the Founder is the oldest painted portrait of the Occident and the most valuable exhibit in Vienna's Cathedral and Diocesan Museum.

AUSTRIA'S ARCHDUCHY

When King Rudolf I enfeoffed his sons Albrecht and Rudolf with the duchy of Austria and Styria, he lay the cornerstone for the rule of the Habsburgs in Austria. In the beginning, the Habsburg territories consisted of the duchies of Austria – roughly modern-day Upper and Lower Austria – and the duchy of Styria. In 1135, the Habsburgs secured the duchies of Carinthia and Carniola and, in 1363, the earldom of Tyrol. These estates, which approximate modern-day Austria without Salzburg, were named the "Austrian hereditary lands". Accession to power of the respective ruler took place as part of a ceremony, which was called an "act of homage".

In 1365, Rudolf IV made the duchy of Austria an archduchy through the forgery of the *Privilegium Maius* by using the made-up title "archduke", which upgrades the basic title of duke and was supposed to ensure him pre-eminence above all other sovereigns of the empire. However this was not recognised until only about one-hundred years later, when, with Frederick III, the first Habsburg was elected emperor of the Holy Roman Empire and he recognised the document forgery virtually on his own behalf.

The original archducal hat of the 14th century no longer exists. The crown, donated by Archduke Maximilian III in 1616 as a votive offering to the Klosterneuburg monastery, remained; it is still there today. Until the proclamation of the Austrian Empire in 1804, the archducal hat was used by all of Austria's regents during the act of homage ceremonies, that is, at the accession to power of the Austrian territories.

Above: The act of homage of Emperor Joseph I in September 1705 in the Knights' Room at the Vienna Hofburg.
Below left: The Privilegium Maius stipulated the archduke's title and, among other things, the indivisibility of the Habsburg territories and the right of primogeniture.
Below right: The Privilegium Maius. Front page of the copy made for Emperor Maximilian I in the year 1512.

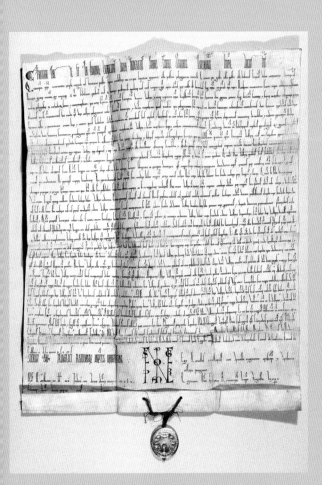

FREDERICK III
THE ENTIRE WORLD IS SUBJECT TO AUSTRIA

In 1440, when Frederick (1415–1493) was elected German king by the prince-electors and was then crowned emperor in 1452, a new era began for the House of Habsburg. From this point onwards, the emperorship, except for a short period in the 18th century to the end of Holy Roman Empire in 1806, stayed in the family. As the only Habsburg, Frederick managed to be crowned by the Pope in Rome. He also founded a determining tradition for the Habsburgs, which meant that the future emperor – mostly the oldest son – was elected by the electors not after death but already while the reigning emperor was still alive.

Lasting 53 years, Frederick's reign may have been unusually long, but it wasn't particularly successful. The majority of it was shaped by conflicts that Frederick was only able to successfully win because he was lucky to outlive his childless adversaries. Firstly his brother, Albrecht VI, who fought the weak emperor; later the Hungarian king, Matthias "Corvinus" Hunyádi, who also attained the Bohemian crown and followed the ambitious plan of uniting both kingdoms with Austria. Matthias even managed to win a few Austrian cities – among them Vienna – for himself. However Corvinus died in 1490 leaving no heirs, which meant that Frederick was able to regain the territories. Frederick seems to have been interested in astronomy and astrology much more than in politics. He had observatories built in the Linz castle, where he lived from 1489; was interested in mathematics, mineralogy, magic and mysticism; maintained contact with alchemists and was interested in the manufacturing of all kinds of miracle substances and healing potions.

His motto "AEIOU", with which he annotated not only his personal objects but also papers and buildings that were important to him, to this day remains a mystery. Up to now, the meaning has still not been clarified. The most well-known interpretations are "Austria erit in orbit ultima – Austria will be the last (surviving) in the world" and "All the world is subject to Austria". The newest research, however, assumes that a magic formula lies behind this enigmatic motto – because Emperor Frederick was intensively involved in magic and mysticism.

When Emperor Frederick died in 1493 at the age of 78, he had, however, accomplished a politically pioneering connection – namely the marriage of one of his sons to Maria of Burgundy, which signified the Habsburgs' rise as one of the leading dynasties.

Above: Emperor Frederick III's motto "AEIOU", with which he annotated not only his personal objects but also papers and buildings that were important to him, to this day remains a mystery. Up to now, the meaning has still not been clarified. The most well-known interpretations are "Austria erit in orbit ultima – Austria will be the last (surviving) in the world" and "All the world is subject to Austria". The newest research, however, assumes that a magic formula lies behind this enigmatic motto – because Emperor Frederick was intensively involved in magic and mysticism.
Left page: In 1452, Frederick III was the first Habsburg to be crowned emperor. Hans Burgkmair the elder, Art History Museum Vienna.

THE HOLY ROMAN EMPIRE

The Holy Roman Empire was founded on Christmas Eve in the year 800, when the Franconian king Charles the Great was crowned emperor by Pope Leo III in Aachen. The Holy Roman Empire – the sobriquet "German Nation" was not used until the Baroque era – was founded by Charles as a supranational empire. Its name came from the aspiration of the Middle-Age rulers to uphold the tradition of the antique Roman Empire and to legitimate the rule as God's holy will. The Holy Roman Empire was an elective monarchy. As laid down in the so-called "Golden Bull", the king was elected the king of the Romans by seven chosen prince-electors: three spiritual – the bishop of Mainz, Cologne and Trier – and four temporal – the king of Bohemia, the margrave of Brandenburg, the count palatine of the Rhine and the duke of Saxony – and then crowned emperor by the pope. Only one single Habsburg – Frederick III – was crowned in this tradition by the pope in Rome. Because the Venetians made the journey to Rome impossible, Frederick III's successor Maximilian had to detour via Trent; Charles V to Bologna, and from the 17th century onwards, the emperor coronations all took place in Frankfurt.

Although the Holy Roman Empire was an elective monarchy, from Frederick III onwards, the electors invariably agreed on a Habsburg – with one exception. When the Habsburgs' male family line ended with the death of Charles VI in 1740, his daughter Maria Theresa would have been next-in-line in the Austrian hereditary lands of Hungary and Bohemia. However, as a woman she was not eligible to become empress of the Holy Roman Empire. The electors thus chose a Wittelsbacher. When he died shortly thereafter, the Habsburgs had such a stronghold that Maria Theresa's husband Francis Stephen of Lorraine was elected and the emperorship again went to the Habsburgs after a three-year intermezzo. The Holy Roman Empire remained upstanding until 1806, when it was dissolved by Emperor Francis II under pressure from Napoleon's claim to power, as well as the founding of the Confederation of the Rhine.

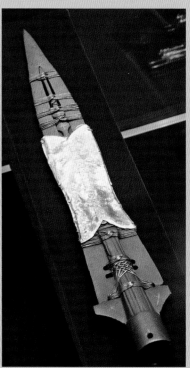

Above: The coronation cloak from the year 1133/34 was worn at coronations until the dissolution of the Holy Roman Empire.
Right: The Holy Lance, for a long time the most distinguished imperial reliquary, symbolised dominance and reliquary at the same time due to an iron pin that is embedded in its blade. This, according to lore, dates back to the Cross of Christ.

Above: The imperial coronation carriages were probably built for Emperor Charles VI around 1735/40. The carriage, drawn by eight white horses, represented the power of the Habsburg dynasty and was only used at the highest-ranking events such as coronation ceremonies.

Leftt page, above: Due to its multi-layered symbolism, the imperial crown from the second half of the 10th century outshone all other crowns. Its octagonal shape refers to the heavenly Jerusalem; the enamel depictions on the panels and the inscriptions contain predicates about governance as well as the virtues of the emperor. The cross stands for the meaning of Christian belief and refers to the self-confidence of the medieval rulers endowed with the divine right of kings.

The globus cruciger was the symbol of world domination. Adding the cross in Early Christian times, the orb became a symbol of Christianity and thus came to stand for the rule of Christ over the world as it was known.

The Imperial Cross from 1024/1025 also had several functions and was not only a symbol of power but also a reliquary. Its shaft has room to store the Particle of the Cross and the Holy Lance.

MAXIMILIAN I
TU FELIX AUSTRIA NUBE

Following the death of his father Frederick III, Maximilian (1459–1519) assumed the rule of the hereditary lands and became king of the Romans in 1493. Because the hostile Venetians made travelling to Rome for the coronation impossible, in 1508 he became "emperor elect", which would then be used by all emperors of the Holy Roman Empire.

Maximilian "The Last Knight" accomplished the rise of Austria due to an equally clever and lucky marriage policy. The strategy of marrying politically to not only expand their own territorial dominion but also to increase the associated political power and wealth became a trademark of the Habsburgs: "Bella gerant alii – tu felix Austria nube! – Let others wage war, but thou, happy Austria, marry!" In 1477, Maximilian himself married Maria of Burgundy, the then richest heiress in Europe. For Maria was not only the heiress to the duchy of Burgundy but also to the Netherlands, through which two economically and culturally blossoming countries fell to the Habsburgs. Many traditions that were then and even today considered

typically Habsburgian or Viennese have their roots in this Burgundian inheritance. This includes what was later called the "Spanish" court ceremonial and the founding of the court choir and orchestra with its still existing tradition of the Vienna Boys Choir. Maximilian married off his son Philip the Handsome to the heiress of the Spanish crown, Joanna the Mad, through which the Habsburgs also inherited the kingdom of Spain with the newly discovered territories overseas. This policy was also consistently upheld in the next generation.

In 1515, through the double marriage of his grandson Ferdinand and his granddaughter Anna to the heirs to the throne King Ladislaw Jagiellos of Bohemia and Hungary, Maximilian secured the option of also appropriating these two powerful kingdoms. This time the Habsburgs were also "lucky" because the Hungarian king, Ludwig II, died in the battle of Mohács in 1526, which meant that both kingdoms in fact fell to the Habsburgs. So, within two generations, Maximilian I managed to secure the requirements for a Habsburg world empire.

Above: After the death of the Duke of Burgundy, Charles the Bold, in January 1477, Maximilian rushed to Brussels to court the heiress of the wealthy country. The marriage to Maria of Burgundy took place in August 1477 and secured the Habsburgs the wealthy inheritance. After falling from a horse, Maria died from a miscarriage in 1482.
Left page: Due to his love of tournaments Maximilian was given the nickname "The last Knight". Portrait by Bernhard Strigel, about 1500.

The double marriage of the emperor's grandchildren, Ferdinand and Anna, with the Hungarian king's children, Anna and Ludwig, on 22 July 1515 in Vienna St Stephen's Cathedral laid the foundation for the inheritance of the Bohemian and Hungarian kingdoms.

The Hungarian St. Stephen's crown is now in the Hungarian parliament in Budapest.

The Bohemian Wenceslas crown is kept in the Vitus Cathedral in Prague.

MAXIMILIANVS. I. IMP.
ARCHIDVX AVSTRIÆ.
DVX BVRGVNDIÆ.

PHILIPPVS HISP. REX.1.
ARCHIDVX AVSTRIÆ.

MARIA DVCISSA
BVRGVNDIÆ MAX: VXOR

FERDINANDVS. I. IMP.
ARCHIDVX AVSTRIÆ.

CAROLVS. V. IMP.
ARCHIDVX AVSTRIÆ.

LVDOVICVS REX
HVNG MASE

The painting of Emperor Maximilian with his family by Bernhard Strigel illustrates the rise of the Habsburgs as one of the leading European dynasties. Left is Emperor Maximilian; outer right, his wife Maria of Burgundy next to their son, Philip the Handsome, who was married to the Spanish heiress Johanna the Mad. Below are Philip's son Ferdinand; in the centre, Charles, and outer right, his son-in-law and heir to the Hungarian and Bohemian thrones, Ludwig Jagiello. When Ludwig fell during battle in 1526, the Habsburgs also inherited the kingdoms of Hungary and Bohemia.

Above: While still alive, Maximilian ordered for his tomb the construction of 40 larger-than-life-sized bronze figures, which were supposed to depict members of his family, ancestors and historical personalities who were seen as symbols of Christian belief. It wasn't until he was on his deathbed that he determined as his burial place St. George's chapel in Wiener Neustadt. Because the figures turned out to be too heavy for the chapel, Maximilian was buried there, but what turned out to be 28 cast figures were grouped around the empty cenotaph in the Hofkirche in Innsbruck. The impressive tomb was eventually given the colloquial name "Schwarzmander" (black men).
Right: Reduction of the figure of the grave of Emperor Maximilian in the Hofkirche in Innsbruck.

THE ORDER OF THE GOLDEN FLEECE

The most prestigious order of the empire originated with the Duke of Burgundy Philip the Good, who established it in 1430 as a knights' brotherhood and friendship alliance for his most distinguished peers of the country. The idea behind it was to defend the honour of God and Christian belief. Philip's main motive, however, was to bind the most illustrious of his empire in an order of chivalry to himself and his house. The members were obligated to absolute fidelity to the order's sovereign. For the "noblemen of name and coat of arms" on the other hand, membership was a distinction – to be accepted into the elite circles of the duke. The wealth and renown of the Burgundian dukes led to the Order of the Golden Fleece becoming the highest rank under the Christian order and, under the Habsburgs as emperors of the Holy Roman Empire, would also keep its importance.

The name of the order originally came from Philip's love of Greek mythology. It originates from the Argonauts legend of Jason, who stole the Golden Fleece, the fleece of the golden ram Chrysomeles, from Colchis (modern day west of Georgia). Over time however, the old myth was consciously displaced by the biblical miracle story of Gideon and the Golden Fleece, because the Christian character of the order was supposed to be emphasised.

When Maximilian I married Maria of Burgundy the Habsburgs became the order's sovereign and remain so still today. The original number of 24 members was finally increased to 70; currently the order has 51 members.

The necklace of the Order, which was worn by the respective emperor of the order as order sovereign, is made up of the symbolic elements flint and fire-steels in the centre of which the Golden Fleece hangs. Flint and fire-steels and what results when the two are used together had been the symbols of the dukedom of Burgundy's reign since Philip the Good and, since the founding of the order, had been the symbols of the order along with the fleece of the golden ram.

CHARLES V
THE EMPIRE IN WHICH THE SUN NEVER SETS

Maximilia's grandson and successor, Charles V (1500–1558), was born in the Flemish city of Gent and raised after the untimely death of his father, Philip the Fair, as his successor in the Burgundian dominions in Brussels. In 1516, however, Charles moved to Spain, where he assumed the rule of his Spanish grandfather, Ferdinand of Aragon, and shortly thereafter, also his mother's, Johanna of Castile and, as first Spanish king, united both the kingdoms of Castile and Aragon. In 1519, when his paternal grandfather, Emperor Maximilian, also died, he united for the first time the kingdoms of Bohemia, Hungary and Spain with his wealthy colonies in South America, the duchy of Burgundy and the Austrian hereditary lands and also ruled as emperor of the Holy Roman Empire. He had become the first Habsburg to have created a world empire, in which the "sun never set". Charles V's reign, however, was marked by a few conflicts. Firstly by the war against the Reformation, but also against France and the Ottoman Empire. These wars were not only financed by the immense wealth exploited from

the Spanish colonies in South America to Europe but also, mainly by the well-off mercantile family of the epoch: the Fuggers.

Charles was able to expand the Habsburg's territorial empire, yet not his actual goal as deeply religious Catholic and emperor of the Holy Roman Empire, whose real task was to defend the Catholic belief. Luther's teaching found more and more followers; the Reformation spread and Charles saw himself as having failed in what was for him the most important challenge. Plagued with burdens, disillusioned and tired of ruling, he abdicated his Spanish title to his son Philip II in 1556. He gave the emperorship and rule of Austria, Bohemia and Hungary to his younger brother, Ferdinand I. With that, Charles V created two lines of the Habsburg dynasty – the Spanish, with residence in Madrid, and the Austrian, which upheld the emperorship, with Vienna as its seat of power. Two years later, Charles died from fatal malaria in the San Yeronimo de Yuste monastery and was buried in Escorial.

Above: Charles' motto was "plus ultra – further beyond" and was illustrated by the Pillars of Hercules, which symbolised the promontories of Ceuta and Gibraltar, which in mythology stood for "end of the world". Charles used it to illustrate his claim to the world supremacy of the Habsburgs.
Left page: Emperor Charles V, portrait by an unknown artist after a painting by Titian. Collection Schloss Ambras, Art History Museum, Vienna.

In the Battle of Lepanto, the largest battle from the galleys in history, the Holy League, commanded by Don John of Austria, defeated the Ottomans in 1571, thus securing supremacy in the western Mediterranean.

Don Carlos, the oldest son of King Philip II of Spain, Alonso Sanchez Coello, ca. 1560.

Philip II, son and successor to Charles V in his Spanish territories, continued the expansion policy of the Habsburgs. He not only ruled as king of Spain, to which the Netherlands, Sicily and Burgundy belonged, but from 1580 also as king of Portugal. In addition to the existing colonies in South America, the Spanish Habsburgs not only conquered Peru, Mexico and Florida, but also the Philippines, which were named after him. His half-brother, Don John of Austria, whom he acknowledged in 1554, played an important role in his victories. Philip II's early death led to speculations about his supposed attempted murder, just as in the case of Philip's son, Don Carlos. Philip had had is son imprisoned for high treason, and a few months later, he died in isolation.

Left: The Spanish monastery and royal palace San Lorenzo de El Escorial near Madrid was built by Charles' son Philip II, who continued the Spanish line of the Habsburgs, between 1563 and 1584, and became the residence of the Spanish kings.

FERDINAND I, MAXIMILIAN II AND RUDOLF II
THE WAR AGAINST PROTESTANTS AND THE OTTOMANS

The successors to Charles V, firstly his brother Ferdinand (1503–1564) and then Ferdinand's son Maximilian II (1527–1576), reigned during a time that was shaped by confessional unrest. Despite Ferdinand and above all Maximilian II not only having come to an arrangement with the Protestants but, like Maximilian, sympathizing with them, the responsibility as emperors of the Holy Roman Empire was still to encourage the Counter-Reformation.

In financial trouble due to the wars with the Turks, Maximilian II accorded the enormous amount of 2.5 million guilders to the religion concession against the resistance of the Catholics, which made it possible for the nobility knighthood to freely enact the Augsburg Confession. Maximilian's dedicated, compensatory and tolerant politics, however, met with disapproval not only in the family but primarily within the empire.

When Maximilian II died in 1576, great hopes were set on his son and successor, who was precautiously brought up in the devoutly Catholic Spain. This had several reasons. On the one hand, it was to strengthen the connection between the Spanish and Austrian lines; on the other, the children were to be brought up strictly Catholic and to incorporate the aloofness and stiff dignity considered important characteristics for an emperor. However, Rudolf II (1552–1612) was to exhibit the negative characteristics of many of the Habsburgs: the emperor was indecisive and

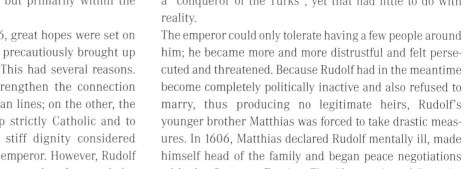

was inclined to depressions, which developed into severe psychological disorders. In 1583, he moved his residence to Prague, where he was less interested in politics than in art and science.

In addition to the war against the Protestants, in the southeastern region of the empire another trouble spot had developed that would threaten the whole of Europe as well as the Habsburg countries for centuries: the war against the Ottoman Empire whose endeavour it was to expand their territories. However the emperor exhibited increasing difficulties in dealing with government business; manic phases interspersed with completely lethargic ones. Severe depression, which increased to perception disorders and schizophrenic episodes, made Rudolf increasingly unfit to govern. He stylised himself as a "conqueror of the Turks", yet that had little to do with reality.

The emperor could only tolerate having a few people around him; he became more and more distrustful and felt persecuted and threatened. Because Rudolf had in the meantime become completely politically inactive and also refused to marry, thus producing no legitimate heirs, Rudolf's younger brother Matthias was forced to take drastic measures. In 1606, Matthias declared Rudolf mentally ill, made himself head of the family and began peace negotiations with the Ottoman Empire. The "fraternal strife" in the House of Habsburg, which also found its way into literature

Above: Emperor Rudolf II moved the Habsburgs' residence from Vienna to Prague and lived in the Prague castle on the Hradčany.
Left page: Rudolf II called leading artists and scientists of the time to his court, and was one of the Habsburgs' first great art collectors. Portrait by Hans von Aachen, 1606/1608.

with the drama of the same name by Franz Grillparzer, ended up in Matthias' favour. In 1608, he became King of Hungary and in 1611 was crowned king of Bohemia; his imperial brother in the Hradčany was only tolerated.

When Rudolf died in 1612, Matthias also succeeded him as emperor. The religious conflict again came to a head and peaked in 1618 with the outbreak of the Thirty Years' War, which would be about the supremacy in Europe. The war raged mainly in Germany, and not only destroyed the country through plundering and marauding droves of soldiers but decimated the population in the German states from 17 to 8 million through starvation and epidemics. The Peace of Westphalia treaty signed in 1648 brought new order to Europe, which meant the collapse of the imperial centralism. The Peace of Augsburg treaty was reinstated and the reformed confessions were acknowledged as equal. The reformed north of the Netherlands retired from the empire and was thus lost to the Habsburgs. Yet the Habsburgs celebrated dynastic success in 1620 with the Battle of White Mountain, in which they conquered the Bohemian Protestants and Bohemia became a hereditary kingdom of the Habsburgs.

The archduke family of the future emperor Maximilian II, Giuseppe Arcimboldo, ca. 1559. On the left is Maximilian's wife, Maria of Spain; in the red dress, her son Rudolf. In 1564, Maximilian succeeded his father Ferdinand I as emperor and, due to his Protestant sympathising, was treated with suspicion by his family.

Emperor Matthias as a young archduke. Painting by Lucas van Valckenborch, ca. 1580. Matthias had his mentally ill brother, Rudolf II, who in the end was incapable of ruling, declared insane and took over government business.

Emperor Rudolf II at a drinking spa. Painting by Lucas van Valckenborch, after 1593.

Defenestration of Prague on 23 May 1618. The catalyst for the move of the Protestant resistance in the Prague Castle was a violation of the religious freedom guaranteed by Emperor Matthias. In an impromptu court hearing, two royal governors and the secretary of the Bohemian chancellery were thrown out the window. The Defenestration of Prague marked the beginning of the uprising of the Bohemian Protestants against the Catholic Habsburgs, and was the catalyst for the Thirty Years' War.

THE HABSBURGS:
COLLECTORS AND ART PATRONS

Over centuries, the Habsburgs distinguished themselves as being great art collectors and patrons and thus came to own one of the largest and most important art collections in the world. One of the first great patrons and collectors was Emperor Rudolf II, who not only collected art by contemporary painters like Correggio and Parmigianino but also brought many famous artists of his time – among them Bartholomeus Spranger and Arcimboldo – to his court. One of his most important purchases was certainly the great Bruegel collection worldwide, which is still located in Vienna today. The emperor placed even greater importance on his art and cabinet of curiosities with valuable work of goldsmiths and stone cutters, but also artfully collected curiosities from exotic or unusual materials like narwhale horns or gastroliths of ruminant animals, which were thought to have healing and miracle effects.

The foundation of the Habsburg art collection was the collection of Rudolf's nephew Archduke Leopold Wilhelm (1614–1662), who as governor of the Netherlands mainly acquired Dutch and Venetian painters and other Italian masters. This is how main works of Giorgione and Tizian, among others, came into Habsburg possession, which thus represented one of the most valuable art collections of the 17th century.

When Leopold Wilhelm returned to Vienna his collection encompassed 1,400 works, which were housed in the Stallburg of the Vienna Hofburg. Over the decades and centuries, the collection was constantly expanded so that main works by Dürer, Velázquez, Titian, Veronese, Tintoretto, Caravaggio, Rubens, Rembrandt and Van Dyck came to join those of Bruegel in Vienna. Today all these art works can be viewed in the Museum of Art History on the Vienna Ringstrasse, one of the most important museums in the world.

Archduke Leopold Wilhelm visits his painting collection in Brussels with his gallery director, the painter David Teniers, ca. 1650.

One of the most important Habsburg art treasures is the largest Bruegel collection in the world. It includes the Tower of Babel by Pieter Bruegel the Elder from the year 1563.

The salt cellar by Benvenuto Cellini – the so-called Saliera – from around 1540 is one of the most important pieces of goldsmithery of the time and is one of the most precious art treasures of the Art History Museum in Vienna.

LEOPOLD I
TURKISH WARS AND BAROQUE FESTIVITIES

Emperor Leopold I (1640–1705) had originally been destined for a clerical career and was educated accordingly. However the early death of his older brother had him moved up in the line of succession. His rule was thus characterised by his piety, which differentiated him from most of the absolute rulers of his time. Yet the emperor was entirely shaped by the Baroque spirit of self-expression and art of presentation, and made the Viennese court a cultural centre of Europe. In order to more tightly bind the high nobility to himself he tried to enhance the status of the Viennese court similar to the "Sun King" Ludwig XIV's by, on the one hand, creating attractive and lucrative positions in the court's administration and in the empire, thus also drawing the empire's nobility. He also organised court life with Baroque splendour and pompous festivities. As an enthusiastic musician, Leopold also fostered the music tradition, loved Italian opera and hired the best composers, musicians, librettists, choreographers and costume makers at enormous cost for his magnificently staged performances. His political successes not only included defending Vienna at the second siege of the Turks in the year 1683, which saw the century-long threat against entire Europe finally averted, but also, thanks to his genius commander Prince Eugene of Savoy, saw the banishing of the Turks from territories in Hungary which had been occupied since 1526. Crucial here was the victorious battle of Zenta in 1697. The subsequent Treaty of Karlowitz in 1699, which brought the acquisition of the whole of Hungary as well as Transylvania and Slavonia, finally saw the Habsburgs' ascent to great power.

Leopold began to transform Vienna into a Baroque city and used many magnificent buildings and monuments as architectural landmarks for the Counter-Reformation, which experienced its heyday under the deeply religious Leopold.

In 1700, when the death of King Charles II ended the Spanish line of the Habsburgs, Emperor Leopold claimed legacy for the Austrian line, although Charles had named his great-nephew Philip of Bourbon-Anjou as his heir in his testament. This resulted in the War of Spanish Succession (1701–1714), the final outcome of which Leopold did not live to see: he died in 1705 leaving the throne to his eldest son Joseph I (1678–1711).

Above: The Habsburgs' rule was closely connected with the Catholic Church, and the Habsburgs were the most important proponents of the Counter-Reformation. Here they tried to win the people back to the "only true faith" using more subtle tactics: with ceremonious processions, resplendent church services and opulently and expensively outfitted churches as well as magnificent buildings that were supposed to impress the people. One such structure is the plague column on the Graben in Vienna. Its clear message was that nothing other than the Catholic faith had conquered the plague.

Left page: Leopold I in theatre costume. The emperor was not only a music lover who primarily patronized Italian opera, but also himself a talented composer. He played several instruments and conducted his chamber orchestra himself. He left behind over 200 compositions – from oratorios to ballets and German singspiele.

Left: Marriages between the Austrian and Spanish line of the Habsburgs were not uncommon and were usually arranged by the parents during their children's childhood. So that the Vienna court could follow the development of Leopold's bride, the Spanish Infanta Margarita Teresa, several portraits by the court painter Diego Velázquez were sent to Vienna.

Right: Emperor Leopold surrounded by his family. His oldest son, Joseph I, died of small pox in 1711 after only a short reign; he was succeeded by his younger brother Charles VI. Geras Abbey, painting by an unknown artist.

Below: On the occasion of Leopold's marriage to the Spanish Infanta Margarita Teresa a horse ballet was performed on 21 January 1667 in the Inner Burghof of the Hofburg. Over 300 dancers and riders and over 200 singers and musicians performed in the bombastically staged celebration. As the Spanish ambassador reported, "a saeculis nix solches gesehen worden – Nothing like this has been seen in a long time".

Chara Musta:
Anno 1683 den 12
aber widerdeniz
Spott Weck geschlagen

Tha Türckischer Groß Vezier welcher
Tülÿ die Kaÿ: Residenz Statt Svien Belagert
Er: mit verlüßt vnd großer
Worden

Above: The decision in the relief battle of Vienna on 12 September 1683 brought Polish troops under King Jan Sobieski, who had joined the allied imperial army in forced marches. Already before the siege, Emperor Leopold had fled from Vienna.

Right: The Turkish horse tail crowned with a crescent was used as a standard of the Ottoman army and also symbolised military grade.

Left: After the bitter battle, the Ottoman army under the leadership of Grand Vizier Kara Mustafa had to admit defeat to the attack by allied troops and, on the evening of 12 September 1683, hastily ended the siege of Vienna. Upon orders of the sultan, Kara Mustafa was strangled with a silk cord in Belgrade for his loss.

PRINCE EUGENE "THE NOBLE KNIGHT"

Although he wasn't Austrian, Prince Eugene of Savoy went down in Austrian history as the most famous commander of the House of Habsburg and great victor over the Turks. He was born in 1663 in Paris, the son of the Prince of Savoy and the Olympia Mancini, a niece of Cardinal Mazarin. Prince Eugene grew up in the environment of the French court in Versailles and in his earliest youth aimed at a military career, despite the fact that his dainty stature – the prince was only 1.61 metres tall – wasn't that of a great warrior. However, the prince was persevering, and when the "Sun King" Ludwig XIV rejected Eugene for service in his army, Eugene offered his services to the emperor of the Habsburgs. Leopold I gave him a chance and wouldn't regret his decision.

At his very first battle, the Battle of Vienna in 1683 as part of the second Turkish siege, Eugene proved his unusual capabilities. His strategic and tactical genius helped him to establish a career very quickly, and only a few years later he became commander-in-chief in Hungary. Under his leadership the Habsburgs were able to banish the Ottomans from Hungary once more. These politically important victories not only made Prince Eugene Lieutenant General and thus Commander-in-Chief of the imperial troops and member of the Geheim Rat (Privy Council) and one of the most important men of the empire, but also one of the richest.

Prince Eugene loved ostentatious representation, had magnificent palaces and castles built by some of the most famous architects of his time; owned one of the then most

Above: Based on a folk song about the conquering of Belgrade, Prince Eugene received the popular nickname, "The Noble Knight".

Below left: The apotheosis of Prince Eugene of Balthasar Permoser in the gold cabinet of the Lower Belvedere.
Below right: In 18th century, the sphinxes in the Belvedere castle gardens were not only considered a symbol of immortality, but due to their meaning as guards of Olympus, the summer residence of the self-assured prince was supposed to be seen as equal to the same.

From 1714, the Lower Belvedere was built by Johann Lukas von Hildebrandt as the prince's summer residence. In 1721, he began with the construction of the Upper Belvedere with its unique view of Vienna, which was exclusively used for the prince's magnificent parties.

valuable art collections and was famous for his glittering parties. Because the prince remained unmarried and childless his entire life, after his death in 1736, his immense fortune went to his niece, Victoria of Savoy. Victoria sold a large part of this inheritance to Emperor Charles VI – including the palace Belvedere in Vienna and Schlosshof in Marchfeld, among others – and a large part of his art collection, which made it Habsburg family property.

CHARLES VI
THE LAST HABSBURG

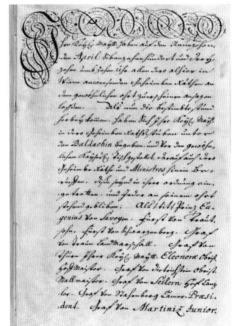

Charles VI (1685–1740) grew up in Spain and was supposed to take over the kingdom of Spain from King Charles II, who was not expected to produce any heirs. However, after Charles II's death, France also laid claim to the Spanish crown, which led to the War of Spanish Succession – at first a success for the Habsburgs. However when Charles' older brother, Emperor Joseph I, died unexpectedly in 1711 and he succeeded him as emperor of the Holy Roman Empire, the situation changed. For in Charles VI, the Spanish and Austrian line of the Habsburgs would have been united in one person, which the other great powers found to be too great a concentration of power. So Charles lost his supporters in the battle against the Bourbons and, in 1714, had to relinquish the kingdom of Spain; only the Spanish neighbouring Milan, Naples, Sardinia and the southern Netherlands (today's Belgium) fell to the Habsburg empire. After returning to Vienna, Charles set about newly regulating the inheritance of the Habsburg countries. In order to secure the succession ahead of that of his older brother Joseph I, Charles issued the Pragmatic Sanction of 1713 in which he declared the Habsburg countries indivisible – thus unifying the Habsburg monarchy for the first time. Furthermore, he secured female succession, a provision whose recognition became more and more desperate since Charles "only" had daughters. Up until his death, Charles' politics was dominated by the upholding of the Pragmatic Sanction. In order for it to be acknowledged by all European powers he was prepared to make many compromises. In the end, however, all his efforts proved to be in vain for, despite the sanction, his daughter Maria Theresa had to fight hard for her inheritance. Prince Eugene, who had urged the emperor to leave her a well-equipped army rather than "a piece of paper", was to have his fears proven right.

Under Charles' rule, Baroque art experienced its zenith, and Vienna finally developed into a Baroque city with numerous magnificent buildings, which dominate the city today. During this time, Charles' court architect, Johann Bernhard and his son Joseph Emmanuel Fischer von Erlach, built the representative parts of the Hofburg such as the Winter Riding School and the Austrian Imperial Court Library, now the Austrian National Library but also numerous churches, like the Karlskirche.

With Charles' death in the year 1740, the male line of the Habsburgs ended, and his daughter, Maria Theresa was left with a heavy legacy.

Above: Emperor Charles VI's most important political objective was the recognition of the so-called Pragmatic Sanction, which made female succession in the Habsburg lands possible.
Left page: Emperor Charles VI, Johann Gottfried Auerbach, ca. 1735.

Emperor Charles grew up in Madrid and took the loss of the kingdom Spanish very hard. Modelled after the Escorial, he wanted to develop Stift Klosterneuburg west of Vienna as a similar monastic residence. Construction of it, however, was only a quarter realised; only two of the domes decorated with the Habsburgs' crown resemble Charles' ambitious plan.

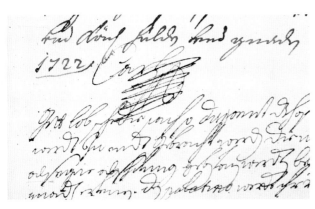

Above: A gracious imperial handwritten letter by Emperor Charles VI, dated 29 June 1722 to the dean of the faculty of law and court commissioner for the Hungarian Reichstag, Johann Georg von Mannagetta, brought the recognition of the Pragmatic Sanction to a conclusion.

Right: Built between 1729 and 1735, the Winter Riding School has been the home of the Spanish Riding School Lipizzaner since Charles VI.

Left page: Between 1721 and 1735, Charles VI commissioned his court architects Johann Bernhard and his son Joseph Emmanuel Fischer von Erlach to build the Court Library. Housed in the Prunksaal, in which architecture, sculpture and painting are united in a Baroque Gesamtkunstwerk, is Prince Eugene's library, acquired by the Habsburgs after his death. The statue of Emperor Charles VI stands in the middle as Hercules of the muses.

THE KAPUZINERGRUFT

Originally the Habsburgs were buried in the royal crypt of St. Stephen's cathedral. From the 17th century, however, the Habsburgs preferred the crypt in the Capuchin monastery on Neuer Markt as their last resting place; it then became the largest and most important imperial tomb. The Kapuzinergruft was founded in the year 1618 by the wife of Emperor Matthias, Empress Anna, who wanted to be buried in the monastery of her confessor, a Capuchin father. She was to be followed by 146 Habsburgs, which is why, over the centuries, the crypt had to be repeatedly extended. According to tradition, during the embalming of the dead, the corpse was divided into three parts and the body, internal organs and the heart were buried separately: the organs in St Stephen's, the hearts in the Augustinerkirche, which was also served as the Habsburgs' wedding church, and the bodies in the Kapuzinergruft. The dead were buried in simple wooden coffins outlaid in magnificent sarcophagi made of tin and, from 1790 onwards, copper. The imperial crypt impressively shows that the representation of the rulers went far beyond death. Mainly in the Baroque era, the sarcophagi also represented the symbol of the power of the dead and were decorated with all the secular insignias as well as symbols of eternal rule. The last Habsburg to be buried in the imperial crypt was ex-Empress Zita, the wife of the last Austrian emperor, Charles I, in 1989.

Right page, above: The magnificent sarcophagus of Emperor Charles VI. Shields and skulls that wear the four crowns of the emperor symbolise the global power of the monarch. The crowns of the Holy Roman Empire, the Hungarian St Stephen's crown, the Bohemian Wenceslas crown and the crown of Castile are depicted. Because Charles could never overcome the loss of the Spanish kingdom, he had the Spanish crown mounted on his sarcophagus. On the grave lid, the grieving Austria together with a Genius hold the emperor's laurel leaf-crowned locket picture, crowned with a self-devouring snake symbolic of eternity. Left are the archducal hat – the insignia of the Austrian archduchy – and the Order of the Golden Fleece. On the right, the imperial orb, the sign of Roman imperial dignity.

Below: According to Maria Theresa's wishes, she was buried with her husband Francis Stephen in a double sarcophagus made by Balthasar Moll. Self-confidently, together with her husband, she holds the sceptre as a symbol of imperial honour.

Left: View from the Maria Theresa crypt to the Charles crypt.
Below: Emperor Francis II/I rests in the Kapuzinergruft between his four wives: Elisabeth Wilhelmina of Württemberg, Maria Theresa of Naples-Sicily – with whom he had three children – Maria Ludovika Beatrix of Modena and Karolina Augusta of Bavaria.

MARIA THERESA
WE MUST HAVE SPECTACLE

In 1740, when Maria Theresa (1717–1780) succeeded her father as Archduchess of Austria and Queen of Hungary and Bohemia at the age of 23, she was first forced to defend her inheritance against the Prussian king, Frederick II, who was allied with France and Spain. In the ensuing War of Austrian Succession that lasted until 1748, Maria Theresa was proved successful, only losing the wealthy Silesia, which fell to Prussia.

After securing her position, Maria Theresa set about modernising the country and became one of the most popular figures in Austrian history. She introduced forward-looking reforms such as general compulsory education, modernised the justice system, abolished torture and forced back the almost absolute power of the sovereigns and classes in favour of a central administration – which in the first instance benefitted the peasants, who had been suppressed and exploited up to that point. In doing so, she was advised by the most famous reformers and scientists in their fields, among them Frederick Wilhelm von Haugwitz, Joseph von Sonnenfels and Gerard van Swieten.

Maria Theresa placed great importance on her family life. Her marriage to Francis Stephen of Lorraine was – unusual for the time – a marriage of love, and Maria Theresa loved her husband until his unexpected death in the year 1765.

To marry Maria Theresa, Francis Stephen renounced Lorraine but in return received Tuscany. Because Maria Theresa as a woman couldn't become empress of the Catholic Holy Roman Empire, after the death of her father, a Wittelsbacher was named emperor. By the time he died in 1745, Maria Theresa had consolidated her power to such an extent that her husband had to be named emperor. Emperor Francis I, however, left the ruling to his wife and was mainly involved, with great aptitude, with the House of Habsburg's finances.

The imperial couple had 16 children and, in contrast to other monarchs of their time, the parents spent an unusually large amount of time dealing with the upbringing of their children, of which 11 reached adulthood. Characteristic for the Viennese court was the passion for theatre and opera. Since the 17th century, the Habsburgs had fostered a particular enthusiasm for theatre performances in which they also actively took part as actors, dancers and singers. Participating in theatre, opera and ballet performances was a fixed component of the royal children's upbringing and thus the family's every day. Performances in which the children of the imperial couple and members of other noble families appeared on stage were almost a daily event and Maria Theresa loved to organise them herself. Participation of the royal children in these

Above: On the occasion of the second marriage of her oldest son, Joseph II, Maria Theresa's three youngest children danced the ballet "Il trionfo d'amore": Ferdinand Carl (b. 1754), Maximilian Francis (b. 1756) and as young Amor, his sister Maria Antoinette (b. 1755), Johann Franz Greippel, about 1765.
Left page: Maria Theresa reigned from 1740 to 1780 as Archduchess of Austria, Queen of Hungary and Bohemia. Because in 1745 her husband, Francis Stephen of Lorraine, was elected Emperor of the Holy Roman Empire, she also carried the title of Empress. Martin van Meytens, about 1750.

"spectacles" alongside the general entertainment also had a pedagogical purpose; from an early age they were supposed to get used to an audience; to speak and to learn good enunciation and, through fun activities, get used to their representational tasks.

When her husband Emperor Francis I of Lorraine died in 1765 completely unexpectedly, Maria Theresa suffered under the early death of her husband and thereafter only wore black. She had not only lost her husband, whom she had dearly loved until his death, but also her best friend and closest confidant. As the first ruling woman of the dynasty, Maria Theresa is still regarded as one of the most popular Habsburgs and is considered a symbol of an energetic but at the same time motherly monarch.

Maria Theresa had the difficult task of combining her role as monarch and mother of 16 children, whereby she firstly saw herself as regent of Austria and secondly as mother. Maria Theresa, who herself had fought for her great love, Francis Stephen of Lorraine, was uncompromising with her own children. For Maria Theresa, the interest of the state was always paramount and she saw the continuation of the traditional marriage policy as her duty as a good monarch. Painting by Martin van Meytens, 1754.

Maria Theresa and Francis Stephen with the young heir to the throne, Joseph, surrounded by her advisors.

The re-conquest of Bohemia in December 1742 was a decisive victory in the Austrian War of Succession against Prussia and was celebrated by Maria Theresa with a ladies' carousel in the Winter Riding School at which she herself and the ladies of her court danced quadrilles with horse and carriage and also competed in skill contests. Painting by Martin van Meytens.

THE IMPERIAL SUMMER RESIDENCE SCHLOSS SCHÖNBRUNN

In the year 1693, Emperor Leopold I. contracted Johann Bernhard Fischer von Erlach to build a hunting castle, which was constructed on the foundation walls of the Lusthaus that was destroyed by the Turks. In the mid 18th century it was expanded by Nicolò Pacassi because Maria Theresa made the official summer residency of the court from April until October out of what was originally conceived as a private palace, and moved her entire royal household from the Hofburg to Schönbrunn.

Dating back from this time are also the magnificent Rococo interiors, still maintained today, and the palace park grounds, which house the oldest zoo in the world. The park's name comes from the legend surrounding Emperor Matthias I, who during a hunt, is supposed to have discovered a clear fountain, the "schönen Brunnen" ("beautiful spring").

Below: Following the death of her beloved husband Francis I Stephen of Lorraine in 1765, Maria Theresa had the emperor's workroom refurbished as a memorial room. The most valuable Chinese black lacquer panels were inlaid in the walnut panelling and embellished with gilt frames.
Above right: The forecourt of Castle Schönbrunn, Bernardo Bellotto, known as Canaletto, 1759/60.
Below right: In the Great Gallery, 40 meters long and 10 meters wide, is where the glamorous festivities of the court – galas, receptions and balls – were held.

Above: The round Chinese cabinet was used by Maria Theresa for secret conferences. Chinese decors with lacquered panels and porcelain vases were very fashionable in the day. Particularly sophisticated was the construction of a hydraulic platform, which made it possible to lower the middle of the floor and to raise a laid table without the servants having to enter the room.

Right page, above: Because in old age Maria Theresa suffered under the summer heat, she had the rooms on the ground floor on the garden side of the palace decorated with illusionist exotic landscape painting by Johann Wenzel Bergl.

Right page, below: The fountain figures of the Roman Ruins in the Schönbrunn Schloss park.

THE HABSBURGS' BARTERED DAUGHTERS

In the marriage of the imperial daughters, exclusively political and dynastic imperatives were crucial. Maria Theresa was well aware that these political marriages often brought the greatest unhappiness for their daughters. About Archduchess Maria Josepha, who was to marry Ferdinand of Naples, a man known to be uneducated, coarse and repulsive, she said: "I look upon poor Josepha as a sacrifice to politics. If only she fulfils her duty to God and her husband and attends to the welfare of her soul, I shall be content even if she is not happy." Her reasons for this were by no means due to lack of love, but, rather, political necessity. For maintaining power and expanding the power of the dynasty – and that was the highest priority – marriage policy was essential. What was the deciding factor was solely the geo-strategic advantage of a marriage; feelings or personal fate played no role at all.

The youngest daughter, Marie Antoinette, who after marrying the future Ludwig XVI lived at the French court, suffered the most under the unbroken paternalism of her mother. That the marriage was not consummated for many years and no heir to the throne was in sight made Maria Theresa increasingly nervous and fretful. In every letter, Marie Antoinette had to explain exactly how she and the king lived, and whether there were any signs of pregnancy. The empress rebuked her daughter for her lavish lifestyle, her craving for pleasure and the wrong choice of her closest surroundings. But above all, she harried her daughter about spending more time with her husband and to make herself "pleasant and indispensible" – for it was the most important job of a queen to bring forth heirs into the world. Marie Antoinette finally bore two children, but was imprisoned during the French Revolution and, in 1793, was sentenced to death and was guillotined. Painting by Élisabeth Vigée-Lebrun 1783.

Left: Maria Theresa's oldest daughter, Maria Anna, had a hunch back and wasn't able to marry. The alternative – that is, going to a convent – was still less of a punishment than emancipation. In the case of the imperial daughters, this did not mean an austere life behind cold convent walls., They were seen as abbesses often in name only, lived in the respective apartments, were, like Maria Anna, able to pursue their scientific interests and probably even lived a much more interesting and more pleasant life than the daughters who were far away from their home and who were primarily there to bring as many offspring as possible into the world.

Right: Maria Theresa was not only a dominant mother but also preferred some children over others, of which she made no secret. Her declared favourite daughter, Marie Christine, who was the only one of her children who was allowed to marry for love, supported by her mother, and married Albert of Saxony. She lived with him as governor of the Netherlands in Brussels. Albert's art collection – today's Graphic Collection in the Albertina – is one of the largest graphic arts collections in the world.

In her instruction for her daughter Maria Amalia, who married the Duke of Parma who was five years younger than her, Maria Theresa wrote: "You know that we must subordinate ourselves to our husbands. We owe obedience; our only ambition shall be in all things of our spouse. We shall serve him and be useful. We shall make our best companion out of him and constantly see in him our lord and master ... You must invest genuine effort to do right by him in your houses, so that he need not go elsewhere to feel comfortable ... Everything is dependent on the woman ..."

JOSEPH II
THE ENLIGHTENED EMPEROR

Already as a young archduke, Joseph (1741–1790) was in blatant opposition to court life and to the "degenerating aristocratic society". He despised all etiquette and preferred a simple lifestyle. After the death of his father in 1765, he became emperor of the Holy Roman Empire and co-regent with his mother Maria Theresa. This co-regency conjured up innumerable discord between mother and son. Maria Theresa was still strongly influenced by the intellectual world of absolutism her son a supporter of the rationally shaped enlightenment. Besides the generational difference was also the meeting of two totally different characters, who both remained consistently loyal to their views. It wasn't until the death of Maria Theresa that Joseph was able to implement his reforms to the degree that they fit his ideas of an enlightened state.

In 1781, he rescinded the serfdom of the peasants and issued the Patent of Tolerance, which secured the free practice of Protestant, Jewish and Orthodox religions. One of his most important projects was the foundation of the General Hospital *(Allgemeines Krankenhaus)*, which was opened in Vienna in 1784 and, of its time, was an exemplary institution of medical care for the citizens. In the terms of admission Joseph declared that "no person, regardless of which nation or religion he may be, shall be denied entry into the General Hospital."

Joseph also opened many Viennese parks and green areas, among them the Schloss Schönbrunn park and the Vienna Prater, which up to then had been open only to the imperial family. Because the idea of usefulness was always paramount to his reforms, all religious orders, except for contemplative ones, were dissolved – which brought him harsh criticism from the Pope.

Because Joseph didn't assume sole sovereignty until very late, many of his reforms came in a hurry and met with major rejection. Mainly his burial regulations, which not only legally regulated the number of candles but also even the use of reusable "economy coffins" and shaft tombs for six people each, were largely rejected by the public and had to be quickly withdrawn.

Joseph didn't have his own family. His first wife Isabella of Parma died after a few years of marriage; their two daughters, already in childhood. His second marriage to Josepha of Bavaria bore him no children. Joseph, having only married her very reluctantly upon "orders" by his mother, avoided any contact with his second wife and even had connecting doors between his and her apartment walled shut. In the year 1790, aged 59, the emperor died of tuberculosis.

Above: The coronation of Emperor Joseph was held on 3 April 1764 in the presence of his father, Emperor Francis I Stephen in Frankfurt.
Left page: Emperor Joseph reigned in the spirit of the Enlightenment and founded numerous social and highly modern institutions like the "Allgemeine Krankenhaus".

Above: Leopold with his family in the garden of the Palazzo Pitti in Florence. The younger brother, Joseph II, resided in Florence as Grand Duke of Tuscany, reformed the country according to the principles of the Enlightenment and made it the first state without the death sentence and tax equality. Painting by Johann Joseph Zoffany, 1776.
Right: Emperor Joseph with his younger brother, Leopold. Pompeo Batoni, 1769. Following Joseph's early death, Leopold returned to Vienna and assumed rule in 1790 as Leopold II. As early as two years later he died without being able to realise his ambitious liberal programme, the model for which he had already established in Florence.

Left page: The marriage of Joseph and Isabella of Parma in 1760 was to be one of the most glamorous festivities of the Viennese court in the 18th century. Alone Isabella's entrance to Vienna with over 90 magnificent carriages was a huge spectacle, which was followed by numerous parties such as the magnificent dinner in the Redoutensäle. Martin van Meytens, after 1760.

FRANCIS II/I
AUSTRIA BECOMES AN EMPIRE

Succeeding Leopold II after his death was his son Francis II (1768–1835), who had inherited little of the liberal spirit of his father and uncle, Joseph, with whom he had grown up. As a consequence, Francis followed a reactionary type of politics that was shaped by the altercation with Napoleon. At first, Francis II reacted to the coronation of Napoleon Bonaparte, who crowned himself emperor of the French in 1804, by proclaiming Austria an empire, as whose first emperor he named himself "Francis I". As Napoleon made his intensions of acquiring the crown of the Holy Roman Empire ever clearer, and the members of the newly formed confederation left the national association, Francis disbanded the Holy Roman Empire in 1806. With that, the history of the empire founded by Charles the Great in 800 came to an end after 1000 years.

Seeing that the Habsburgs couldn't do much against the French emperor in a military way, and Napoleon conquered great parts of Austria and even occupied Vienna in 1805 as well as 1809, they fell back on their well-tested marriage policy. In 1810, Marie Louise, the daughter of Emperor Francis, married Napoleon, for whom this connection was likewise very important. He desperately needed an heir to the throne, with which his wife Joséphine de Beauharnais was not able to provide him, and the connection to the most important European dynasty.

Following Napoleon's defeat, from 1814 for half a year, Vienna became the centre of European politics when the ruling governors of all powers came to the imperial city in order to draw up the new borders to Europe at the Vienna Congress. At this summit of European powers, Vienna experienced glittering parties, receptions and balls under the supervision of the powerful Austrian state chancellor Klemens Wenzel Lothar Prince Metternich, which led to the saying "The congress does not run; it dances". Also after the congress, Metternich determined the reactionary politics of the Viennese court, which strictly suppressed national and liberal currents and tried to maintain the balance of power in Central Europe.

When Emperor Francis died in 1835, his son Ferdinand took over the rule.

Above: Emperor Francis II/I with his fourth wife, Carolina Augusta of Bavaria, his grandson, the Duke of Reichstadt, his daughter-in law, Archduchess Sophie, his daughter Marie Louise, his oldest son and successor, Ferdinand and his second-born son, Archduke Francis Charles. Painting by Leopold Fertbauer, 1826.
Left page: As Emperor of the Holy Roman Empire he bore the name Francis II. After the dissolution of the empire in 1806, as first Austrian Emperor, he called himself, Francis I. Painting by Friedrich Amerling, 1832.

Left: In 1810, Marie Louise married Napoleon and became empress of the French. Following his defeat, she left him and went to Parma, which in the course of the Vienna Congress had been awarded to her as a duchy. After Napoleon's death she married again twice, had another three children and died in Parma in 1847.

Right: The son born to Napoleon and Archduchess Marie Louise in1811 came to Vienna after the fall of his father and grew up with his grandfather, Emperor Francis. He received the title Duke of Reichstadt and died as early as 1832, aged 21, from laryngeal tuberculosis.

Below: Francis and Napoleon after the Battle of Austerlitz. Painting by Antoine-Jean Gros.

At the Congress of Vienna, the Habsburgs lost the southern Netherlands (today's Belgium), but, with the newly acquired Kingdom Lombardo-Venetia and with Parma and Tuscany, were even able to build on their supremacy in Upper Italy.

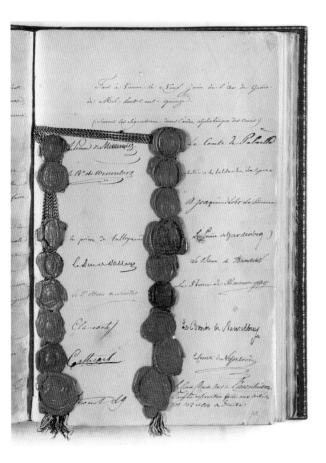

Above: In 1809, Archduke Charles was the first commander to defeat Napoleon on the open battlefield near Aspern. That shortly thereafter Napoleon would defeat the Austrians again and previously had even "conquered" Vienna, did not dampen the popularity of the archduke – he received an impressive equestrian sculpture on the Heldenplatz in Vienna.
Left: The final act of the Vienna Congress was signed on 9 June 1815. State Chancellor Prince Metternich signed for Austria; for France, Foreign Minister Count Talleyrand; for Prussia, Wilhelm von Humboldt.

Francis I on his return to Vienna after the Battle of Leipzig. Johann Peter Krafft, 1833.

THE AUSTRIAN EMPIRE

The Austrian Empire was founded in August 1804 by Archduke Francis as a hereditary national empire. Until the dissolution of the Holy Roman Empire in the year 1806, Francis carried both imperial titles and called himself Francis II/I. After that, as Emperor Francis I, he only carried the Austrian imperial title. Because the imperial title was hereditary, a coronation ceremony was not necessary; the insignia was the magnificent house crown of Emperor Rudolf II, which thus became the Austrian imperial crown. The Austrian empire existed as a unified ruling structure until 1867, when, as part of the Compromise with Hungary it became the Austrian-Hungarian K.u.K. – that is, imperial and royal – dual monarchy.

The crown of the Austrian empire, the private crown of Emperor Rudolf II, which he wore at official occasions, was made in Prague in 1602 by Jan Vermeyen, the most important goldsmith of his time. The crown of the Holy Roman Empire was exclusively worn at the coronation ceremony and otherwise, according to tradition, kept by the City of Nuremberg.

Above left: Emperor Francis' second daughter, Leopoldina, married the Portuguese Crown Prince, Dom Pedro. She followed him to Brazil, where he was crowned emperor of Brazil. Abused by her violent husband for years, Leopoldina died at the age of 30 from a miscarriage, which was caused by a hefty kick from her husband to her stomach.

Above right: From 1835, the successor to Emperor Francis I was his oldest son Ferdinand "the Benign", who was unable to rule due to his severe case of epilepsy. He left government business to his State Chancellor Metternich and in the end abdicated in the course of the bourgeois Revolution of 1848 in favour of his nephew Francis Joseph. He then lived in Prague, from where he administered the manors of his nephew, the late Duke of Reichstadt, and thus amassed a private fortune, which he bequeathed to his nephew and successor, Francis Joseph.

Right: The younger brother of Emperor Francis II/I, Archduke John of Austria, was one of the most talented Habsburgs. He supported the liberal powers in the country and was elected regent in the course of the 1848 French Revolution by the Frankfurt National Assembly and thus the first head of state to be elected by a parliament. After the Revolution failed, he retired from government in 1849. After years of fighting, his imperial brother approved his marriage to his great love, the postmaster's daughter Anna Plochl. He lived in Styria, where he brought about a huge economic upswing through modernising the industry, promotion of the railways but also culture and education.

FRANCIS JOSEPH I
VIRIBUS UNITIS

When Francis Joseph (1830–1916) was born, there was no way to be certain that he would one day become the emperor of Austria and thus the regent of the second largest country in Europe after Russia, with 52 million subjects. However his ambitious mother, Archduchess Sophie, hoped that her son would become successor to the ill Emperor Ferdinand I, and she scrupulously prepared Francis Joseph for this task. From earliest childhood, "Franzi" was virtually "trained" to be the emperor and complied with the plans of his mother.

Finally, when, as part of the Bourgeois Revolution of 1848, Ferdinand had to abdicate, Sophie had achieved her goal. Her husband and the younger brother of the emperor, Archduke Francis Charles, waived their rights to the throne, her son Francis Joseph became emperor of Austria at the age of 18.

The beginning of his reign was characterised by military conflicts. First of all, Francis Joseph brutally quashed the uprising of the Hungarians, which he first succeeded with the help of the Russian tsar Alexander II and which made him extremely unpopular in Hungary. In the war against France in 1859, Lombardy and, after the Habsburgs' loss at the Battle of Königgrätz 1866 against Prussia, and in the end not only the supremacy in the German Federation, but also the last Italian province – Venetia – were lost. This debilitation led to negotiations with Hungary and ended in 1867 with the so-called Compromise (*Ausgleich*) demanded by Hungary, which was the founding of the Austro-Hungarian dual monarchy.

Francis Joseph ruled a multinational monarchy, whose national territories comprised today's states of Austria, Hungary, the Czech Republic, Slovakia, Slovenia, Croatia, Bosnia-Herzegovina and parts of modern-day Poland, the Ukraine, Romania, Montenegro, Serbia as well as northern Italy. An empire in which 10 languages were spoken and which the growing nationalism increasingly caused concern. Emperor Francis Joseph may have shaped the history of Europe during this epoch, however he did not distinguish himself as one of the most politically important monarchs – actually, quite the opposite. His reign was characterised by his holding on to old-school and bureaucratic performance duties. Part of his popularity had to do with the long duration of his rule. Francis Joseph died in 1916 at the age of 86 following a 68-year reign.

Above: Coat of arms of the Austro-Hungarian dual monarchy created in 1867.
Left page: Emperor Francis Joseph in gala uniform, Francis Xaver Winterhalter, 1865.

Left page, left: Until her death in 1872, Archduchess Sophie, who had fought for her son Francis Joseph to become emperor, remained one of his closest confidants and most important political advisor.

Left page, right: The young Archduke Francis Joseph with his brothers, Ferdinand Max, the future emperor of Mexico and Charles Ludwig.

Left page, below: The imperial family on the Schönbrunn castle terrace. The only original photo of the imperial family shows, sitting in front: Empress Elisabeth with her children Gisela and Rudolf; beside them, Archduchess Sophie; standing behind, Emperor Francis Joseph with his brother Ferdinand Max and his wife, Charlotte; Ludwig Viktor and Charles Ludwig; sitting down, his father Francis Charles.

Right: On 2 December 1848, Archduchess Sophie's life's ambition was fulfilled: her son Francis Joseph became emperor to Austria.

Below: Excursion of the bridal couple Francis Joseph and Elisabeth on the day of their engagement, 19 August 1853, in the environs of Bad Ischl, Gottlieb Prestl, ca. 1855.

THE AUSTRO-HUNGARIAN DUAL MONARCHY

Through the Compromise with Hungary in 1867, the Austro-Hungarian monarchy was founded, which was also called the "K.u.K. monarchy" for "imperial and royal". The dual monarchy comprised the imperial Cisleithania, which Austria was officially called until 1915, and the royal Hungarian Transleithania – named after the Leitha mountain range that comprised the border. Head of state was in personal union with the emperor of Austria and apostolic king of Hungary, who was also head of foreign, financial and military politics. All other territories were determined by the independent Hungarian diet.

Below: On 8 June 1867, Francis Joseph was crowned King of Hungary in the Church of St. Matthew on the castle hill in Budapest.
Right: Container of the Hungarian coronation earth. According to ceremony, earth from all counties of the land was brought to the coronation in Budapest by the kings of Hungary in gilded brass containers and emptied on the coronation hill. As part of the ceremony, the king would ride up the hill and, with the symbolic striking of the sword towards all cardinal points, vowed to defend the land against all enemies.

Left: Elisabeth only once got involved in her husband's government business in order to support Hungary. The Hungarians honoured the empress' support by crowning her Hungarian queen together with Francis Joseph and venerated her during her lifetime.
Right: Emperor Francis Joseph in Hungarian uniform.
Below: Castle Gödöllö north-east of Budapest was presented to the imperial couple on the occasion of their Hungarian coronation by the Hungarian nation. The castle became one of Empress Elisabeth's favourite residencies.

IMPERIAL EVERY-DAY – THE IMPERIAL APARTMENTS

Left page, above: Emperor Francis Joseph always felt that he was, firstly, officer of his state; his fulfilment of duty was his utmost priority. His working day began at half-past three every morning. After a short morning prayer, he performed his ablutions in his bedroom at a simple wooden wash basin and a bath in a rubber tub, which was especially brought in, because Francis Joseph rejected having a private bathroom, thinking it an unnecessary luxury.

Left page, below: The emperor began his day shortly after 4 o'clock in the morning at his desk, where he began to work on preprepared documents. His work was interrupted only by a brief lunch, which he took directly at his desk so as not to lose any time. In front of his desk stood his favourite portrait of his beloved wife, Empress Elisabeth.

Right: The family dinners took place in the early evenings, to which family members and guests staying in Vienna were invited. Even the family dinners followed a strict ceremony; one was only allowed to speak to those sitting on either side; conversation with those opposite was not allowed. The meal was transported to the apartments from the court kitchen in warmed boxes and prepared in a room next door. Dinner mostly comprised 9 to 12 courses and usually took roughly an hour.

Below: During carnival in the Hofburg, glittering court balls were held to which aristocrats, diplomats, politicians and artists were invited. The "Waltz King" Johann Strauss conducted the orchestra as Hofkapellmeister and played his beloved waltzes.

For Francis Joseph, the Kaiservilla in Bad Ischl was his "earthly heaven" to which he was able to flee, as he himself described best "from the paper desk-existence filled with worries and troubles", each summer. Here, every year on 18 August, the imperial family also celebrated Francis Joseph's birthday.

Francis Joseph's greatest passion was hunting, during which he could relax in nature. However he wasn't a trophy collector but a true hunter. He loved to go deer stalking and, up to a ripe old age, was still able to trek for up to one-and-a-half hours to the towers and always wore his rifle himself while doing so.

Above: Emperor Francis Joseph with his grandson at Easter. As strict as Francis Joseph was as a father, he strove touchingly as a grandfather. Mainly with the children of his daughter Marie Valerie, he spent a lot of time on Schloss Wallsee in Lower Austria. He loved the role of "Opa-pa", which the children called him, and played with them for hours. "The children are his greatest friends – he even rolled around on the floor for Ella", wrote his daughter in her journal.

Right: Francis Joseph's only vice was smoking. So that the cigar smoke didn't bother anyone, he used a cigar holder made out of meerschaum.

Below: In later years, his few private hours included a daily visit from his long-time friend and confidant, Katharina Schratt. The Burg Theatre actress, with her humorous and warm-hearted way, was soon accepted and acknowledged at the court as well as by the family as "the girl-friend". After all, Empress Elisabeth herself had introduced Katharina to the emperor and hired her as a reader. She knew that her husband was in good hands with the cheerful actress, and thus secured herself another piece of independence.

EMPRESS ELISABETH
TITANIA SHALL NOT GO WHERE PEOPLE WALK

From the first day, Elisabeth (1837–1898), who had just turned 16 on 24 April 1854, married her cousin, Emperor Francis Joseph, felt uncomfortable in her role as empress of Austria. At first she tried to fulfil peoples' expectations, however her duties as empress were uncomfortable from the beginning. Appearances as well as the strict court ceremonials were increasingly tiresome and she abhorred the inflexible hierarchical structures and intrigues of the Viennese court.

At representational functions she felt, in her own words, paraded like a horse "in a harness." Yet Elisabeth, called "Sissi" by the family, with time learned to stand up for herself against the Viennese court. The beautiful empress recognised the power of her beauty, used it for her own personal interests and ended up living a life that fulfilled her expectations only.

Elisabeth was unusually sporty and became one of the best parforce riders of her time. She took extended trips – of which she mainly loved ship cruises where she was at the mercy of the elements. But although she was able to freely organise her life and was everything but caught in a golden cage, she did not find happiness. She refused to fulfil the court-imposed, traditional duties as wife, mother and empress, but didn't seek any other function.

The older she got, the more the empress withdrew, became unsociable and unapproachable. She wrote melancholy poems, indentified with the fairy queen Titania from Shakespeare's "Mid-Summer Night's Dream", and wrote, "Titania shall not go where people walk/In this world, where no one understands her". Following the suicide of her son, Elisabeth only wore black and most people only experienced her as a black silhouette in the distance. Depression and thoughts of death increasingly plagued her.

On 10 September 1898, Elisabeth was murdered by the Italian anarchist Luigi Lucheni in Geneva. When Emperor Francis Joseph received notice from his aid-de-camp Count Paar of his wife's death he said: "You have no idea what this woman meant to me."

Because Elisabeth withdrew very early on from her public role as empress and avoided representational functions she was not at the centre of public interest. In this respect, Emperor Francis Joseph occupied a far more important role. The "good old emperor" was fixed in the hearts of the population; he had their sympathies.

However the situation changed abruptly when, after Elisabeth's murder the "marketing potential" of the beautiful, secretive and above all, tragically killed empress was recognised. Thus, Elisabeth posthumously became a worshipped, selfless empress who was close to the people. A critical debate on her ambivalent personality, her egocentricity and egomania was completely eliminated and thus perpetrated a false image. With Ernst Marischka's "Sissi" trilogy in the Fifties, Elisabeth eventually became the

Above: To stay fit and slim, the athletic empress trained daily in her dressing room, which also functioned as a gym.
Left page: Empress Elisabeth in ball dress with the famous diamond stars in her hair, Francis Xaver Winterhalter, 1865.

worldwide renowned and adored "Sissi". Contributing a great deal to that was the actress Romy Schneider – who to this day shapes the picture of a young, warm-hearted and unconstrained Sissi – yet which has very little of the actual character of the empress Elisabeth.

Below: Empress Elisabeth was considered one of the most beautiful women of her time and was also aware of this. She was particularly proud of her knee-length hair, which was brushed two hours every day.

Left page
Above left: Elisabeth as a young empress, Anton Einsle, ca. 1855.
Above right: Elisabeth was proud of her slim figure, which didn't comply with the beauty ideal of the time – round, voluptuous forms. Above all, she found it extremely important to emphasise her waistline, which measured 51 cm.
Below: Elisabeth distinguished herself as one of the best riders of her time. After years of hard training, she succeeded in being able to not only participate as the only woman at the dangerous parforce hunts in England and Ireland, but also to win them.

Left: Elisabeth on Corfu. Posthumous portrait by Frederick August von Kaulbach, after 1898.

Right page: Elisabeth not only loved Homer and Greek mythology but also generally the culture of Ancient Greece. On the Greek island Corfu she had the Achilleion built – a palace-like refuge that was named after her favourite hero of Greek mythology. It was hardly finished when the restless empress felt burdened by it and sold it again.

Right page, below left: Elisabeth with her court lady Irma Sztáray on 3 September 1898 in Geneva. The last photo of the empress before her death.

Right page, below right: At the age of 60, Elisabeth became a victim of the Italian anarchist Luigi Lucheni, who stabbed the empress with a file on 10 September 1898 in Geneva while she was on her way to the shipping pier.

CROWN PRINCE RUDOLF
I SEE THE SLIPPERY SLOPE DOWN WHICH WE GLIDE

Crown Prince Rudolf (1858–1889), the only son of the imperial couple, was very like his mother in many aspects when he was a child. He had a variety of interests, was inquisitive and sensitive. In order to harden the young heir to the throne for his future role and to prepare him for his military career, the six-year-old was prescribed a strict military education, which made a scared, nervous and sickly child of the sensitive Rudolf, and was to have a deciding influence on his later life.

Without any semblance of pedagogical sensitivity, his educator, Count Leopold Gondrecourt, used draconian measures on the seven-year-old, such as cold-water treatments, drills that lasted for hours under rainy and cold conditions, nightly gun shots to wake the boy and other such things. Francis Joseph loved his son, but found him effeminate and was convinced that the military drills would do Rudolf good. Elisabeth, who in the first few years of Rudolf's life was mostly travelling and during this time only had written contact to her children, had no idea.

Yet when she saw Rudolf in 1865, after being away for a long time, she was so shocked by the condition of her scared and nervous son that she gave Francis Joseph an ultimatum and demanded that Rudolf's educator be changed. The emperor relented and Elisabeth subsequently ordered Count Joseph Latour as the new teacher. Through Count Latour, Rudolf received a liberal bourgeois-shaped education, which made him into an open-minded, inter-ested man, who abhorred the aristocratic way of life. His private environment consisted primarily of liberal, intellectuals and scientists, for which he was severely attacked by the conservative and clerically-minded Viennese court, and he made enemies in politically influential circles.

Rudolf bemoaned the isolated position of an emperor, who only relied on the reports of his advisor, and even only got to read selected newspaper articles. Rudolf's political views became more and more starkly contrasted to the official politics of the Viennese court and forced him to live a life full of secrecies. He encrypted his political correspondence; he published his political articles anonymously.

For years Rudolf fought for a task that suited his abilities, but during his lifetime, was ignored by his father. Francis Joseph had no confidence in his son and let him feel this painfully. In 1881, the crown prince married Stephanie of Belgium; two years later, their daughter Elisabeth, "Erzsi", was born. The marriage, which in the beginning was initially harmonious, over the years, was threatened by the differing personal development of the two as well as increasing debauchery of the crown prince. In the end, it failed not least because he infected his wife with the sexual disease gonorrhoea (the clap) the result of which she could no longer bear children.

From 1888, Rudolf's frame of mind dramatically deterio-

Above: The imperial couple with the crown prince couple in the castle park in Laxenburg near Vienna, Carl Schweninger, 1887.
Left page: Crown Prince Rudolf in hunting costume, photo ca. 1887.

rated. His failed battle for the recognition of his father, his failed marriage and numerous love affairs had made a desperate and resigned person of the 30-year-old Rudolf. To his trusted Count Latour he wrote: *I see the slippery slope down which we glide; am very close to things, but cannot in any way do anything; am not even allowed to speak loudly or say what I feel and think.*

On 30 January 1889, at the hunting castle in Mayerling, Rudolf shot himself along with his last lover, the 17-year-old Baroness Mary Vetsera, who was prepared to die with him.

Above: Empress Elisabeth with her children Gisela and newborn Rudolf, aquarelle by Joseph Kriehuber.
Left: Two-year-old Rudolf with a play-dog.

Below left: Emperor Francis Joseph with his children Gisela and Rudolf.
Below right: Through his educator, Joseph Graf Latour, Crown Prince Rudolf was the first Habsburg to receive a bourgeois-liberal and scientific-oriented education. Painting by Heinrich von Angeli, 1885.

Above: The hunting castle in Mayerling: In the early hours of the morning on 30 January 1889, Rudolf first shot Mary Vetsera and then himself. Because it was supposed to remain a secret that a young girl died with the Crown Prince, Mary's family had to remove the corpse of their daughter from Mayerling under degrading circumstances in secret.

Left: The 17-year-old Baronesse Mary Vetsera was the last lover of the crown prince. The murder and suicide however wasn't a lovers' story. Rudolf didn't want to die alone and, in the rapturous and enamoured Mary, had found someone who was prepared to die with him.

Below: That Rudolf was murdered can be excluded, alone due to the availability of the dated farewell letters. The photo of the laid-out crown prince also proves the fatal head injury due to a gun shot.

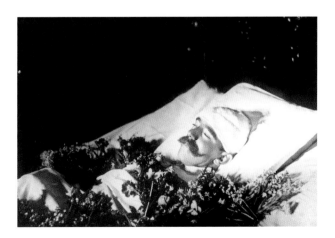

Following the tragic suicide of Crown Prince Rudolf, Francis Joseph's nephew Francis Ferdinand (1863–1914) was named successor. The oldest son of Archduke Charles Ludwig was known to be energetic and direct, but at the same time extremely conservative and one-sided and was thus loved in court circles as well as with the public. From time to time, he had even had differences of opinion with Francis Joseph and when, in 1894, Francis Ferdinand fell in love with Sophie, Duchess of Hohenberg, his relationship to the emperor deteriorated even more. For Sophie was from old, yet not upper, nobility, and was thus not seen as an equal. Francis Joseph refused to endorse the marriage. But Francis Ferdinand fought for his love and, in 1900, was finally successful after he had agreed to a morganatic marriage, the children from which would not be eligible for the throne.

Politically, the heir to the throne, who made no secret of his anti-Hungarian and pro-Czech ideas and thus made enemies on many sides, was active against the court's aggressive expansionist Balkan politics and for the keeping of peace. Unjustly, in public he was considered to be an advocate of anti-Serbian politics and because of this drew hatred from the anti-Habsburg south-Slavic nationalists.

In June 1914, against all warnings, he led the field exercises and manœuvres on the Bosnian-Serbian border. Driving through Sarajevo, the heir to the throne and his wife, who was accompanying him on the trip, were shot on 28 June by the Bosnian nationalist Gavrilo Princip. The fatal assassination of the couple had dramatic consequences. Emperor Francis Joseph, pressed by his political advisors and military, signed an ultimatum to Serbia that was equal to a declaration of war. With this, Francis Joseph led his empire into a world war, which would lead to the collapse of his empire and would cost almost 10 million people their lives.

Left: The car in which the heir-to-the-throne couple was shot shows traces of the bomb attack that had taken place one hour before the fatal shooting. The perpetrators threw a bomb at the car, but at first missed their target.
Right: The uniform of the murdered heir apparent.
Left page: With Sophie, Francis Ferdinand had a happy marriage, which produced three children – Sophie, Maximilian and Ernst. In Vienna the family lived in Schloss Belvedere; summer was spent at Schloss Konopiště in Bohemia and at the family's Schloss Artstetten in the Wachau.

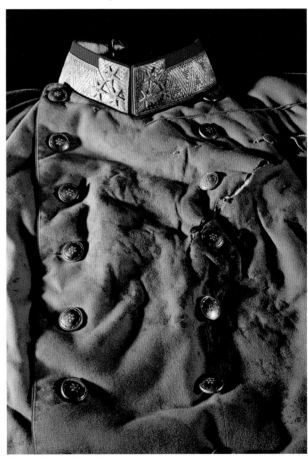

CHARLES I
THE END OF THE MONARCHY

Following the death of the heir to the throne Francis Ferdinand, a great-nephew of Emperor Francis Josephs was determined as his successor. When Charles (1887–1922) became emperor after the death of Francis Joseph in November 1916, Austria had more or less accomplished all its objectives in war. Serbia had been conquered; shortly thereafter, Russia had become so weakened due to the revolution that it wasn't a serious adversary, and the USA had yet to enter the war. Charles' advisers were also convinced that peace had to be urgently declared not only because the situation was favourable, but because major supply problems were looming, bringing with them great danger.

Yet Charles did nothing but continue to decidedly wage war – and with unauthorized means. The twelfth battle of Isonzo, which began on 24 October 1917 with the support of German troops, was only able to be won by using huge amounts of poison gas. The last remains of his credibility to the world community and his ally Germany were lost when his secret dealings about a separate peace for the K.u.K. monarchy were made known. Whether his motivation was the general will for peace or an attempt to save the monarchy is a matter of conjecture.

In any case, in March and May 1917, through his brother-in-law, Sixtus of Bourbon-Parma, he had presented his adversaries a secret peace offering behind the backs of his German allies. The negotiations failed, and in spring 1918, the scandal broke out, when France – provoked by the Austrian foreign minister Ottokar Czernin – published the secret letters, which went down in history as the Sixtus Letters. At first, Charles denied his authorship; but when it was able to be proven, he was seen as a liar and betrayer. The consequence was an act of self-abasement to Spa, with which Charles definitively delivered the monarchy to the German Reich, thus losing not only the last room to manœuvre but also primarily the respect of the allies.

The end of World War I in November 1918 also meant the end of the k. u. k. monarchy and thus the rule of the Habsburgs. The former crown lands formed their own national states. Charles finally signed a relinquishment of administration of the state, but refused to abdicate – which meant that he and his family had to go into exile in Switzerland. Following two attempts from there to reinstate the monarchy in Hungary, he was exiled to Madeira, where he died in 1922 of the Spanish flu.

Above: Emperor Charles during World War I in a Kaiserschützen (Imperial Infantry) uniform.
Left page: Emperor Charles I was beatified by Pope John Paul II in 2004.

On 21 October 1911, Charles married Zita of Bourbon-Parma in Schloss Schwarzau am Steinfeld. The marriage was the last glittering family celebration during the lifetime of Emperor Francis Joseph, who also gave a speech there. Zita was an ambitious and determined woman who would soon

play an important political role. She acted as the most important advisor to her husband, who was challenged in his role as emperor, and was present at all meetings and decisions.

EPILOGUE
THE HABSBURGS AFTER 1918

Due to his refusal to abdicate and to acknowledge the Republic of Austria, Emperor Charles I and his family went into exile. The other members of the imperial family – in the first instance, the direct descendants of Emperor Francis Joseph – forfeited their claim to rule and were thus able to stay in Austria and retain their private assets. According to the peace treaty of St. Germain, a distinction between private and state-owned property was made whereby the "free and personal private assets of the former emperor and the members of the imperial house" remained untouched, whereas the property that the Habsburgs owned in their function as rulers (the so-called "dynastic" property) went to the Republic.

The expropriation of the Habsburgs also included assets that dated back to Francis Stephen of Lorraine's family pension fund, which were defined as dynastic assets and awarded to the successor states as well as the Republic of Austria in the St. Germain treaty. Due to the Habsburgs' waiver, the considerable private fortune of Emperor Francis Joseph, which he had left to his daughters and grandchildren, remained theirs and they were able to remain in Austria while keeping their private assets – numerous castles, manors and estates. With the family of the youngest imperial daughter of Marie

Valerie, most of the direct descendants of Emperor Francis Joseph still live in Austria – so, too, the descendants of his son Crown Prince Rudolf, the family Windisch-Graetz. In total, there are over 300 Habsburgs spread throughout the world. The oldest family member, Dr. Otto of Habsburg-Lorraine, son of the last emperor, Charles I, lived in Pöcking am Starnberger See in Germany and, for many years, was an MP of the Christian Social Union (CSU) in European parliament. After signing the release declaration in 1961, he was allowed to enter Austria again and received Austrian citizenship as well as German. Head of the family since 2007 is his oldest son, Charles Habsburg-Lorraine, who lives in Salzburg and is the president of the Paneuropean Union. Charles' younger brother George, who lives in Budapest, campaigns for Hungary's accession to the European Union and is president of the Hungarian Red Cross.

Most of the Habsburgs are no longer politically active today. Many are involved in international organisations, work as artists and PR consultants. Only the youngest daughter of Otto von Habsburg, Walburga Habsburg Douglas, followed her father as a politician and is an MP in Swedish parliament. Otto von Habsburg-Lorraine died on 4 July 2011, in Pöcking am Starnberger See.

Above: For many years, Otto von Habsburg-Lorraine was a member of the German CSU in European Parliament; he lived in Pöcking am Starnberger See.

Left page, above: The last Austrian imperial couple had eight children. Born in 1912, Archduke Otto signed the waiver in 1961 and was thus able to re-enter Austria.

Left page, below: Otto von Habsburg-Lorraine with his wife Nancy Regina (died in 2010) and three of their seven children. Their remains were buried in the Kapuzinergruft.

Photo credits

The Author

Until 2007, **Katrin Unterreiner** was scientific head of the Imperial Apartments of the Vienna Hofburg and curator of the Sisi Museum. She has had numerous exhibitions (including "Crown Prince Rudolf" and "Empress Elisabeth. Myth and Truth") as well as authored many books on the Habsburgs and publications on the Vienna Hofburg and the every-day culture at the Vienna court.

ISBN 978-3-85431-580-3

styria

© 2011 by Pichler Verlag
in the Styria GmbH & Co KG publishing group
Vienna-Graz-Klagenfurt

Books from the Styria publishing group can be purchased
at all book shops and also from the online shop.

styriabooks.at

Book and cover design: Bruno Wegscheider
Production: Franz Hanns
Translation: Mag. Mý Huê McGowran
Reproduction and image editing: Pixelstorm, Vienna
Printing and binding: Dimograf, Bielsko-Biała, Poland